NOW -I- KNOW
ALL AROUND ME

Sally Hewitt

A **TWO-CAN** book
published by
Thomson Learning

First published in the United States in 1995 by
Thomson Learning
New York

Copyright © Two-Can Publishing Ltd, 1995

Text: Sally Hewitt
Consultant: Alison Ruddock
Illustrations: Amelia Rosato
Editors: Kate Asser and Sue Barraclough
Design: Lisa Nutt
Production: Lorraine Estelle
Photo research: Sam Riley

Photographic credits: Bruce Coleman: 28 BC/Brian Henderson: 42 (tc); BC/Trevor Barrett: 43;
Eye Ubiquitous: 41; Fiona Pragoff ©: 5; Image Bank: 25; John Butcher: 26 (c); Pictor Uniphoto: 32 (c);
Pictures Colour Library: 47; Robert Harding: 12; Steve Shott: 34, p35; Telegraph Colour Library: 29; Tony Stone:
6, TS/Peter Correz: 8, TS/David Hiser: 40; Zefa: 36 (c).

All other photographs: Ray Moller.

Library of Congress Cataloging-in-Publication Data

Hewitt, Sally.
  All around me.
    p.   cm. — (Now I know)
  Summary: Covers a wide variety of scientific facts about the world around us, including
the human body, weather, food, clothing, plants, and animals, with suggested mini-projects.
  Includes index
  ISBN 1-56847-266-8
  1. Scientific recreations — Juvenile literature. 2. Science — Study and teaching (Elementary) — Activity programs —
Juvenile literature. [1. Scientific recreations.] I. Title. II. Series: Now I know (New York, N.Y.)
Q164. H55 1995
372.3 — dc20   95–9050

Printed and bound in Hong Kong by Wing King Tong

Contents

My Body   4

My Senses   6

My Family   8

My Home   10

Growing Up   12

Fun and Games   14

Staying Healthy   16

Things We Use   18

Clothes We Wear   20

Keeping in Touch   22

Weather   24

Green and Growing   26

Food We Eat   28

Shopping   30

Crowded Cities   32

Going Places   34

Jobs People Do   36

Factories   38

Children of the World   40

Homes Around the World   42

Our Earth   44

Out in Space   46

Index   48

My Body

How does my body work? The different parts of the human body work together like an amazing machine. The body never stops, even when you are asleep.

Your **brain** sends messages around your body telling you to feel, think, speak, and move.

Your **heart** pumps blood around your body.

You use your **lungs** to breathe in and out.

In your **stomach**, food is broken down so your body can use it to make energy.

Skin protects your body. It stretches when you move, mends itself when you are cut, and keeps out water and germs.

TRY IT OUT

The parts of your body that bend are your joints. Move them back and forth. Test which of your joints move in a circle.

Food from the stomach moves into the **intestines**, which pass nutrients from the food into the blood.

4

Your **skeleton** is made of hundreds of bones joined together. Bones are strong and hard and give your body its shape.

skull

elbow

wrist

ribs

spine

hip

Your **skull** protects your brain. **Ribs** protect your heart and lungs.

knee

ankle

When you run, you need more oxygen, so your **heart** beats faster and pumps blood around your body more quickly.

Take a big breath to feel your **lungs** fill with air. Then breathe out into a balloon to see how air from your lungs blows it up.

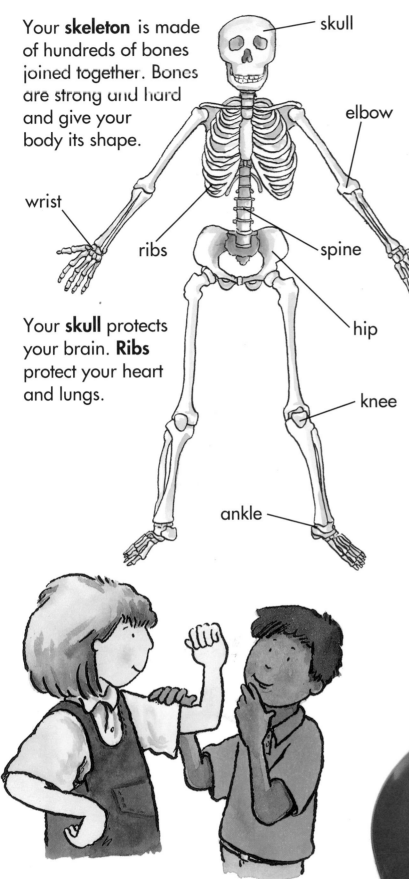

You use **muscles** to move your body. Muscles called biceps bend your arms. When you smile, you use about fifteen muscles!

My Senses

What are my senses?
Your senses help you see, hear, smell, taste, and feel. Without them you would not know what was happening around you. Imagine if you couldn't smell or taste food or feel the warmth of the sun.

You use your eyes to **see** all sorts of things, such as colors, shapes, patterns, pictures, and words.

PLAY IT

Play the senses game! Blindfold two friends and ask them to touch an orange and a bar of soap. Can they guess what they are?

You **feel** through your skin if things are hard, soft, wet, dry, hot, or cold. What does a cat feel like?

Banging drums, barking dogs, and people cheering are just some of the many loud sounds your ears can **hear**.

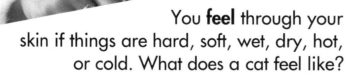

Ask a friend wearing a blindfold to guess what food she is eating. Does it **taste** sweet, sour, salty, or bitter?

Smell and **taste** are closely linked. If you have a cold and cannot smell, you cannot taste well either.

MATCH IT

Look at the objects in the big box. You can see them all, but which other senses do you use? Can you taste, smell, feel, or hear them, too?

hear   feel   smell   taste

Your nose can tell the difference between thousands of **smells**. The scent of flowers is sweet. Can you think of an unpleasant smell?

My Family

Are all families the same?
Some children live in large families with their mother and father, brothers and sisters, and even grandparents, uncles, aunts, and cousins. Other children live in small families with just their mother or their father. Every family is different.

Tom lives with his **mother** and **father**. His parents love and care for Tom and his **sister** Rosie.

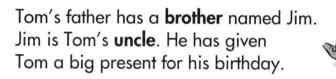

Tom's father has a **brother** named Jim. Jim is Tom's **uncle**. He has given Tom a big present for his birthday.

Tom has two sets of **grandparents**. Grandma and Grandpa are his father's parents. What have they given Tom for his birthday?

THINK ABOUT IT

What color hair and eyes do you have? Do you look like others in your family?

Grandpa

Grandma

Aunt Jo

Uncle Jim

Jane

Lauren

Aunt Sue is Tom's mother's sister. She has a baby named Mary. Tom wants to hold his new **cousin**.

Uncle Jim has **twin** daughters. They were born at the same time. They are Tom's cousins, too.

MAKE IT

Tom has made his family tree. Look at the way he has arranged his pictures.

Set out your family tree in the same way as Tom. Glue the pictures to a big piece of paper.

This is a group picture of Tom's **family**. Can you find Tom and his sister Rosie?

Grandma

Grandad

Dad

Mom

Aunt Sue

Rosie

Tom

Mary

Some **friends** feel as if they are part of Tom's family. Lily and Ari live next door to Tom and spend a lot of time with him.

My Home

What makes your home special? Your home is special because you live there with your family. It is where you sleep, eat, and play. It shelters you from all kinds of weather, and you feel safe there.

PLAY IT

Play the memory game! Draw a chart similar to this one. Then think of a room in your home – but not the one you're in! Draw ten things you will see when you go into that room.

Score one point for each of the things you remembered correctly.

The **bathroom** is where you wash and use the toilet.

A **boiler** heats up water for the sink and shower.

The **kitchen** is where people keep food, cook, and eat. Do you enjoy cooking?

Imagine you can change everything in your bedroom. How would you decorate it?

You sleep, dress, and play in your **bedroom**.

Electricity gives us light and heat. It comes into the house through cables.

A **living room** is a good place to rest, read a book, or watch television.

Growing Up

Will I ever stop growing?
Since you were a baby, your body has changed and grown; and you are still growing now. Think of all the things you have learned how to do. One day your body will stop growing, but there will always be new and exciting things to learn.

Babies crawl around on their hands and knees before they learn to stand up and walk.

These **toddlers** are just learning to talk. They can say simple words, such as *book* and *doll*.

When children are about five years old, they go to **school** to learn how to read, write, and count.

THINK ABOUT IT
Find photographs of your mother and father when they were babies. How have they changed?

12

There are lots of things to learn outside school. Do you know how to ride a **bicycle**?

MAKE IT

See how much you change over time by making a time capsule. Fill it with special things about yourself. Write down your age and height, too.

Put it all in a box and do not open it for a year. How have you changed?

Teenagers learn how to do some of the things that only adults are allowed to do, such as driving a car.

After school or college, people learn how to do a **job** to earn money for food and a home.

Some **elderly people** can stop working. They have money saved up and time to do the things they enjoy most.

Fun and Games

What shall I do today?
Think of all the things you can do and the games you can play, either on your own, with just one friend, or with lots of other people. What is your favorite way to spend time?

These children are **making** a kite. They have paper, glue, paints, scissors, and string.

Do you like **stories**? They can be funny, scary, sad, or exciting. Try making up your own story.

MAKE IT

You can make musical instruments at home.

1 To make a guitar, stretch rubber bands over the hole in an old tissue box.

2 Make a shaker by putting beads in a plastic bottle and putting the lid on.

If you don't have a yard, you can **grow** plants in flowerpots indoors or in window boxes.

Do you enjoy making **music**? You can dance along, too. Get together with some friends to play in a band.

Can you spot three children whizzing around the park on wheels? What are they all wearing to protect themselves if they fall?

Usually **soccer** is a game you play to win, but throwing and catching a Frisbee is just for fun.

There are lots of things you can do on your own, such as painting or flying a kite.

POOL

Where are these children going? What are the clues?

15

Staying Healthy

How do I stay healthy?

You can stay healthy by eating different kinds of food, drinking lots of water, running and playing, and getting enough sleep. Staying healthy makes you fit and strong enough to do and enjoy anything you try.

THINK ABOUT IT

When you sneeze or cough, your body is getting rid of germs and dirt, so make sure you cover your mouth!

When you sweat, your body loses water. **Drink** plenty of water when you play hard.

While you **sleep** after a busy day, your body rests and builds up strength for a new day.

Wash your hands before you eat. If germs on your hands get into your mouth they can make you sick.

cookies

yogurt

milk

cheese

vegetables

bread and cereal

This **food pyramid** shows how much of each type of food you should eat to stay healthy.

candy

eggs, fish,
and meat

fruit

pasta and rice

Choose one person to be mud monster. If the mud monster catches you, you are "stuck in the mud" until another player crawls through your legs.

You should eat plenty of the foods at the bottom and only a little of the foods at the top.

Your **doctor** cares for you when you are sick. She also gives you injections to protect you from diseases.

Did you know your heart is a muscle? **Exercise**, such as running or swimming, works your muscles and keeps you fit.

A **dentist** helps you care for your teeth. You need to brush your teeth properly every day to keep them healthy.

Things We Use

What will I use today?
Whatever you do, you probably use something to do it with. You don't have to think hard about what to use when you brush your teeth. Someone has made something that is just right for the job.

You wake up in the morning when an **alarm clock** rings. Would you wake up without one?

A **teapot** is specially shaped for pouring. How is a spoon specially shaped for eating?

We use all sorts of brushes. A **toothbrush** is just the right size and shape to clean your teeth.

FIND IT

Which of the things on this page do you use? Can you think of any other things you use every day?

Imagine digging without a **shovel**. It would be very hard work. What other tools do you use in the garden?

Cookie cutters are useful tools. Can you see two other tools used in the kitchen?

When you make a model, you use **scissors** for cutting. What else do you use?

When it's dark, we use a **lamp** to give us light.

MATCH IT

Look at these different brushes. Can you say what each brush is used for?

19

Clothes We Wear

What shall I wear today?
You might wear a jacket to go to school or your favorite clothes to go to a party. You need warm clothes on a cold day and waterproof clothes on a rainy day.

Clothes made from **cotton** keep you cool in hot weather. A hat will keep the sun off your head.

Some animals have thick fur to keep them warm. We wear **wool** clothes to keep us warm.

MATCH IT

We wear special clothes at different times. Can you match up the pairs?

A **waterproof** coat, trousers, and boots keep a fisherman dry at sea. How do you stay dry?

It can be very cold or very hot in space, so **astronauts** wear space suits for protection.

Gymnasts wear stretch clothes that don't get in the way when they jump, twist, and somersault.

Soccer players wear colored or patterned shirts to show which team they belong to.

Around the world, people wear different clothes for special occasions. This is a Japanese **kimono**.

FIND IT

Look through this book to find another astronaut wearing a space suit and a rocket-powered backpack.

21

Keeping in Touch

How do we keep in touch?
People use words to keep in touch. We use words to let other people know what we think, how we feel, and what we want, and to ask questions. Words can be joined together to make stories, songs, poems, and jokes. If we cannot speak directly to each other, there are many other ways to keep in touch.

Babies **cry** to tell us what they want because they cannot talk. This baby might be hungry.

Words can be **written** as well as spoken. You can send a card to say "Happy Birthday" to someone you love.

PLAY IT

Play the making-faces game! Show that you are happy, angry, or scared, without speaking.

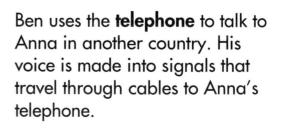

Ben uses the **telephone** to talk to Anna in another country. His voice is made into signals that travel through cables to Anna's telephone.

We watch **television** to learn and for fun. It brings words and pictures from around the world into our homes.

Computers are a sort of electronic brain. Some are linked together and people use them to talk to one another.

Anna's telephone rings when **signals** from Ben's telephone reach it. She picks it up to talk to Ben.

A **radio** lets you hear music and words sent through the air from radio stations far away.

Sometimes people who cannot hear use **sign language** to talk. There are signs for every letter and for most words.

PLAY IT

Without speaking, try to make a friend understand that you want each of these things.

Weather

What's the weather like today?
Look outside! Is the sun shining, or
is it raining or snowing? Is it hot,
cold, wet, or windy? All over the
world the weather is different, and it
changes each day.

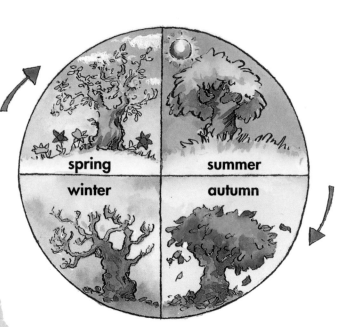

In some countries, the weather
changes each **season.** It's warm
in spring, hot in summer, cool
in autumn, and cold in winter.

Often people travel to hot
countries on **vacation.**
Where have you been on
vacation?

When the sun shines through
raindrops you can see a **rainbow.**
Rainbows have seven colors.

FIND IT

People wear hats in
all kinds of weather.
Look at these pages
to find different hats
to keep you dry and
warm and to protect
you from the sun.

When you are out in the
rain, waterproof clothes
keep you dry. Umbrellas
help, too.

When the air is very cold, it may **snow**. When snow covers the ground, it's time to go sledding!

Wind is moving air. You cannot see it, but you can feel it and see it moving things.

Tornadoes are whirling storms of wind. They race over the land and can cause terrible damage.

25

Green and Growing

What are plants?
Trees, flowers, and vegetables are all plants. There are millions of different types of plants in the world and they grow in all kinds of places, but each one needs water, air, and sunlight to live.

If you plant a sunflower **seed** and water it, soon it will start to grow.

First, the **roots** grow down into the soil, searching for water. Then the shoot grows up toward the sun.

The shoot grows a strong stem and green leaves, and then a tightly packed **bud**.

Soon the bud starts to open and a bright yellow **sunflower** turns to face the sun.

FIND IT

Rabbits like to nibble grass and leaves. Look carefully at these pages. Can you find five rabbits?

Trees are the biggest plants. Some trees lose their leaves in autumn and grow new ones in spring.

GROW IT

Draw a face on an empty egg shell. Fill the shell with wet cotton and sprinkle on some cress seeds. Water the seeds a little each day and watch the cress hair grow.

All plants need **water** to grow, but some plants can grow right in the water.

Some of the **vegetables** we eat are the roots of plants. They grow under the ground.

Food We Eat

Where does all the food come from?
A long time ago, everybody hunted, fished, and gathered plants for food. Today, most people don't have to spend time hunting because large farms and factories make plenty of food, which we buy from stores.

On huge farms in Australia, **sheep** are raised for their wool and meat.

Large crops of **fruit** are usually grown in warm countries. These oranges are ripening in the sunshine.

PLAY IT

Play the fruit game! How many different types of fruit can you think of? Can a friend think of more?

Wheat is grown in big fields. When the wheat is ripe, combine harvesters cut it down. The wheat is ground into flour and made into bread.

Fish from the sea are sometimes caught in large nets pulled along by fishing boats. The fish are put on ice to keep them fresh.

Cows are raised for their milk. Cheese and butter are made with milk.

Free-range **hens** scratch around farms for food to eat. They lay eggs, which the farmer sells.

FIND IT

Look at these different foods. Which two should you eat plenty of, and which two should you eat a little of? You can find the answer in this book.

In some places, people grow their own fruit and vegetables, and raise animals for milk and meat. They sell any spare food at a market.

Shopping

Why do we go shopping?
We go shopping to buy things we need, such as food, clothes, presents, toys, games, and books. You can shop in markets, big department stores, supermarkets, or small local shops.

When you need to buy lots of food and supplies, you go to a **supermarket**. You put your groceries in a cart, then you pay for them at a checkout counter.

Some stores sell one kind of thing. **Toy stores** are full of puzzles, models, toys, and games.

THINK ABOUT IT

If you had $5 to spend, what would you buy? What kind of store would you go to? Would you spend all your money in one place?

When you go to the supermarket, how do you carry the **groceries** home? Do you go by bus or car?

PLAY IT

Here are three things you can buy in stores. The bicycle costs more money than the shirt or the cookie. The cookie is cheaper than the shirt.

If you want to buy just one thing, you might go to a small shop, such as a **bakery**.

Department stores are large and sell all kinds of things, from children's clothes to television sets.

Each day, **markets** are set up and vendors put out their goods to sell.

Crowded Cities

Why are cities so busy?
Millions of people live in a city, and thousands more travel to the city to work or spend the day. All day long, the roads are busy with cars, buses, and bikes. And in the evening, the streets are crowded with people going to the movies and to restaurants.

Trees, grass, and lakes in a peaceful **park** make a change from the noisy streets.

When people are sick or hurt, they go to the **hospital** to be cared for by doctors and nurses.

Many people keep money in **banks**. They can use plastic cards to take money from machines outside the bank.

THINK ABOUT IT

The Earth is so crowded that in the future we could be living in even taller buildings, huge underground cities, or out in space.

Hundreds of people live or work in **office buildings**, which rise above the crowded city and take up only a small amount of land.

These pictures show what happens inside four of the buildings on this page. Can you match each picture to the right building?

There are four movies to choose from at this **movie theater**. What's your favorite movie?

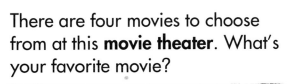

Restaurants serve food from all over the world, including Greek lamb dishes and Indian curries.

Museums display interesting objects such as dinosaur bones, artwork, and rockets.

33

Going Places

How do we travel?
If there were no buses or trains, it would take a long time to travel from place to place! For trips across the world, many people fly in airplanes or go by boat.

Airplanes fly around the world quickly. They fly between airports. Airports have runways, which planes need for taking off and landing.

Ferries are boats that can carry people, cars, trucks, and even trains across rivers and seas.

Cars are a popular way to travel. Before cars were invented, people used horses and carriages.

MATCH IT

Here are four different ways to travel – by road, sea, rail, and air. Match each picture with a vehicle on this page.

Helicopters don't need runways to take off. They can hover in one place and fly in any direction.

FIND IT

Look at all the wheels on this page. Do they all look the same? Which vehicles don't have wheels?

Fire engines carry firefighters and their equipment to put out fires. Their sirens warn other traffic to make way.

Bus passengers can either buy tickets for short trips around town or for longer journeys from city to city.

Big **trucks** have powerful engines and carry heavy goods. Some trucks are shaped to carry special loads.

A **train** can carry passengers, heavy goods, and mail in one journey. The wheels of the train travel along tracks.

Jobs People Do

What shall I be when I grow up? Each day, all around you, people work at different jobs. Who delivers the mail? Who collects your trash? Who works in your school? You could work in an office or a park, on a farm or in a fire station. Which job would you choose?

Chefs cook food in restaurants and hotels. Would you like to cook all day?

Clowns paint their faces and wear funny clothes. A clown's job is to make people laugh.

PLAY IT

Play the jobs game. Pick a job, but don't say which one. Pretend to do the job, without speaking. Can your friends guess which job it is?

A **gym teacher** explains the rules and shows students how to play different sports. Do you enjoy playing sports?

Architects draw plans for builders to follow when they are putting up new buildings.

Construction workers do many different jobs. They start by digging foundations using heavy equipment. They build walls with bricks and cement.

Hairdressers cut and style hair. Do you know that hair never stops growing?

Firefighters rush to put out fires. They use fire engines fitted with ladders and hoses.

MATCH IT

Can you name all of these objects? Match each object to the person who uses it to do a job. You'll find two of the people on other pages of this book.

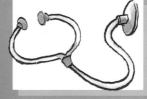

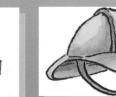

1 Trucks deliver **metal tubes** and other things needed to make the bicycle to the factory.

Factories

What is a factory?

A factory is a big building where teams of people use machines to make lots of one kind of thing. Most things can be made quickly and cheaply in factories. This is how a bicycle is made.

2 Machines cut and bend the metal tubes to make the bicycle **frame**. Other machines spray the frame with paint.

3 Some of the small parts, such as the **brakes** and **seat**, are put together by hand.

FIND IT

Machines are built to make jobs easier. Can you spot a machine on this page that is used for lifting and moving heavy things?

4 **Wheels** are put together bit by bit: first the spokes, then the rims, and finally the tires.

5 The frame is put on an **assembly line**, where workers fit all the parts to the frame.

SORT IT

This wooden train was made by hand. These pictures show how it was made, but they are in the wrong order. Can you sort them out?

6 The bicycle is **tested** to make sure it works properly and is safe to ride.

7 Then the bicycle is taken to a **shop** to be sold. When you ride your bicycle, don't forget to wear a helmet.

Children of the World

How many children are there in the world? There are millions of children in the world. They live in over 190 countries and speak many different languages, but, just like you, they go to school and enjoy playing with friends and dressing up for special days.

Todd lives in New York City in the **United States of America**. After school, he likes to play baseball with his friends.

New York

Statue of Liberty

Sagrada Familia Cathedral

Barcelona

Mexico City

National Cathedral

Marisol lives in Barcelona, **Spain**. She enjoys flamenco dancing. She waves her hands and stamps her feet.

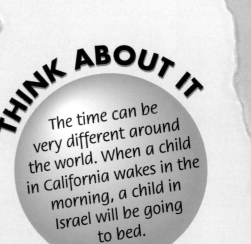

Paolo lives in Mexico City, in **Mexico**. He's wearing an animal costume for a big parade in the streets.

THINK ABOUT IT

The time can be very different around the world. When a child in California wakes in the morning, a child in Israel will be going to bed.

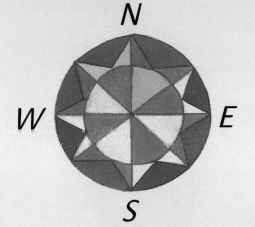

Hanif lives in Lahore in **Pakistan**. His favorite sport is cricket. He likes batting best, but he can bowl, too.

Badshahi Mosque

● Lahore

Beijing ●

Great Wall of China

Chow Wu lives in Beijing, the capital city of **China**. She is wearing special clothes and jewelry for a festival.

Parliament Building

● Nairobi

Sekou lives in Nairobi, in **Kenya**. He has been chosen to play soccer for his school team.

Maggie lives in Sydney, which is the biggest city in **Australia**. On weekends, she likes to surf at the beach.

Sydney Opera House

● Sydney

Homes Around the World

Do all homes look the same?
Some people live in apartments or houses. Some live in homes similar to the ones shown on these pages. All over the world, people live in different kinds of homes built from all sorts of materials, including mud, bricks, and snow.

These houses are built high up on stilts. When there are floods, the houses stay warm and dry.

In hot, dry places some people live in cool **mud houses** with grass roofs.

These nomads are desert people who move from place to place. They live in **tents,** which are easy to put up.

Inuit hunters build **igloos** from blocks of snow, packed tightly together to keep in the heat.

THINK ABOUT IT

Imagine you are a nomad, living on the move. Make a list of all the things you would carry with you.

These **floating houses** may be built from reeds. People paddle the houses to the shore to buy food.

MATCH IT

Who lives where? Can you find the homes of these people and bird in this book?

Homes can be **decorated** in all kinds of ways. This mud house in South Africa is painted in bright colors. Which parts of your home are painted?

Our Earth

What is the rest of the world like? If you traveled around the world, you would go across deep seas and up high mountains. You would see rain forests full of giant trees and flat, open grasslands. Some places would be hot and dry and others icy and cold. In every place, there would be different plants and animals.

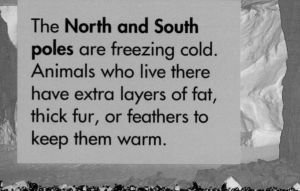

The **North and South poles** are freezing cold. Animals who live there have extra layers of fat, thick fur, or feathers to keep them warm.

Huge numbers of different creatures live in the **sea**. Many stay in shallow, warm water where it is light and plants grow.

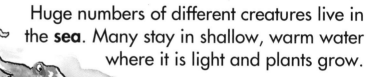

MATCH IT
Where in the world does each of these animals live?

Most of Earth is covered by sea. Imagine traveling all the way around the world without stepping on land!

Hot, wet **rain forests** are teeming with animals and plants. There is always plenty of water to drink and food to eat.

Groups of animals roam across wide open **grasslands**. They move on when they have eaten all the grass in one place.

Mountain animals live in cold rocky places, where there are only a few plants to eat.

Desert people and animals have special ways to survive in their hot, dry home. Some animals come out only at night when it is cool.

45

Out in Space

What is space?
On a clear night you can look out into space. It stretches as far as your eyes can see and much, much farther. Space and everything in it – the stars, moons, planets, rocks, and dust – is called the Universe.

Stars are balls of burning gas. Enormous groups of stars are called **galaxies**. Our sun is a star in a galaxy called the Milky Way.

Earth is the planet where we live. It travels around the sun once every year.

The **space shuttle** carries astronauts into space. It returns to Earth when its mission is over.

The **sun** is the closest star to Earth. It gives us heat and light. Nothing could live on Earth without the sun.

A **rocket** similar to this one carried the first astronauts to land on the moon.

A force called **gravity** keeps your feet on the ground. Without gravity you would float off into space!

There is no air in space, so **astronauts** wear space suits and carry air with them.

MAKE IT

Make a space scene. First, paint a sheet of paper blue. Then cut out planets from colored paper and stars from foil.

Build a spaceship from small boxes to zoom through your space scene. Tape a photo of yourself to the spaceship.

Our **moon** is a ball of rock with no water and no air. It travels around Earth every 29 days.

Index

airplanes, 34
alarm clock, 18
architect, 36
assembly line, 39
astronauts, 21, 46, 47
aunts, 9
Australia, 41
autumn, 24, 27

babies, 12, 22
bakery, 31
bank, 32
bathroom, 10
bedroom, 11
bicycle, 13, 38-39
body, 4-5
bones, 5
brain, 4, 5
brakes, 38
breathing, 4, 5
brother, 8
bud, 26
bus, 35

cars, 34
chef, 36
China, 41
clothes, 20-21, 24
clown, 36
computer, 23
construction worker, 37
cotton, 20
cousin, 9
cry, 22

dairy cows, 29
decorated, 43
dentist, 17
department stores, 31
desert, 42, 45
doctor, 17
drink, 16

ears, 6
Earth, 44-45, 46
elderly people, 13
electricity, 11
exercise, 17
eyes, 6

factories, 38-39
family, 8-9
father, 8
feel, 6
ferries, 34
fire engines, 35, 37
firefighters, 37
fish, 29
floating houses, 43
food, 16, 17, 26, 28-29
friends, 9
fruit, 17, 28

galaxies, 46
games, 14-15
grandparents, 8
grasslands, 45
gravity, 47
groceries, 30
growing,
    plants, 14, 26, 27
    up, 12-13
gymnasts, 21

hairdresser, 37
health, 16-17
hear, 6
heart, 4, 5, 17
helicopter, 35
hens, 29
homes, 10-11, 42-43
hospital, 32

igloos, 42
intestines, 4

jobs, 13, 36-37
joints, 4

Kenya, 41
kimono, 21
kitchen, 10

lamp, 19
lungs, 4, 5

markets, 31
Mexico, 40
Milky Way, 46

moon, 47
mother, 9
mountain, 45
movie theater, 33
mud houses, 42, 43
muscles, 5, 17
museum, 33
music, 14

North Pole, 44
nose, 7

office buildings, 32
oxygen, 26

Pakistan, 41
parents, 8
park, 15, 32
plants, 26-27

radio, 23
rain, 24
rainbow, 24
raindrops, 24, 25
rain forests, 45
restaurants, 33
ribs, 5
rocket, 46, 47
roots, 26

school, 12
scissors, 19
sea, 44
seasons, 24
seat, 38
seed, 26
senses, 6-7
sheep, 28
shoot, 26
shops, 30, 31, 39
shovel, 19
sign language, 23
signals, 22, 23
sister, 8
sitting room, 11
skeleton, 5
skin, 4, 6
skull, 5
sleep, 16

smell, 6, 7
snow, 25
soccer, 15, 21, 41
South Pole, 44
space, 46-47
space shuttle, 46
spade, 19
Spain, 40
spring, 24, 27
stars, 46
stomach, 4
stories, 14
summer, 24
sun, 24, 46
supermarket, 30

taste, 6, 7
teapot, 18
teenagers, 13
teeth, 17, 18
telephone, 22, 23
television, 23
tents, 42
toddlers, 12
toothbrush, 18
tornadoes, 25
toy stores, 30
train, 35
trees, 27
trucks, 35
twin, 9

uncle, 8
United States of America, 40
Universe, 46

vacation, 24
vegetables, 26, 27

wash, 16
water, 10, 16, 27
waterproof clothes, 20, 24
weather, 24-25
wheat, 28
wheels, 35, 38
wind, 25
winter, 24
wool, 20
words, 22